Italian Foods & Culture

by Jennifer Ferro

The Rourke Press, Inc.
Vero Beach, FL 32964

S

Note to Readers: The recipes in this book are meant to be enjoyed by young people. Children should ask an adult for help, however, when preparing any recipe involving knives, blenders, or other sharp implements and the use of stoves, microwaves, or other heating appliances.

On the Cover: *Italians in Palermo take part in a parade celebrating the Festival of Santa Rosalia.*

Photo Credits: Cover photo CORBIS/Vittoriano Rastelli; p. 4 EyeWire; p. 6 Omni-Photo/ Richard Hackett; p. 7 Omni-Photo/Catrina Genovese; p. 8 Fototeca E.N.I.T.-Roma; p. 10, 20, 30 PhotoDisc; p. 12 CORBIS/Jonathan Blair; p. 19, 26, 38 Paul O'Connor; p. 21 Fotocolor E.N.I.T.-Roma; p. 22 AP Photo/Andrew Medichini; p. 31 Lou Dematteis.

Produced by Salem Press, Inc.

Copyright © 1999, by The Rourke Press, Inc.

Library of Congress Cataloging-in-Publication Data

Ferro, Jennifer. 1968-
    Italian foods and culture / Jennifer Ferro.
    p.   cm. — (Festive foods & celebrations)
    Summary: Discusses some of the foods enjoyed in Italy and describes special foods that are part of such specific celebrations as St. Joseph's Day, Christmas, and the Festival of Santa Rosalia. Includes recipes.
    ISBN 1-57103-302-5
    1. Cookery, Italian Juvenile literature. 2. Food habits—Italy Juvenile literature.
3. Festivals—Italy Juvenile literature. [1. Food habits—Italy. 2. Cookery, Italian.
3. Festivals—Italy. 4. Holidays—Italy. 5. Italy—Social life and customs.] I. Title.
II. Series: Ferro, Jennifer. 1968-   Festive foods & celebrations.
TX723.F467   1999
641.5945—dc21   99-21050
                                                     CIP

First Printing

PRINTED IN THE UNITED STATES OF AMERICA

Contents

Introduction to Italy

Italy (IH-tull-ee) is a country on the *continent* (KON-tun-unt) of *Europe* (YUR-up). It is easy to find Italy on a map because it is shaped like a boot. The boot seems to be kicking a ball. This ball is the island of Sicily (SIH-suh-lee). Sicily is also part of Italy.

Italy is made up of 22 different regions. These regions have different foods, different ways of living, and sometimes different languages. In 1870, all these areas came together to form one country.

Food is the biggest part of living in Italy. If you are not hungry, an Italian may tell you to eat something to make you hungry. Cooking and

The Forum was built in Rome thousands of years ago during the Roman Empire.

eating food is very important to Italians. Coffee is the favorite drink of Italy. People drink tiny cups of strong coffee called *espresso* (eh-SPREH-so) all day long.

Many Italians grow vegetables and fruits in their own gardens. People prepare delicious food with them.

Italians celebrate many holidays. Most of them are related to the four *seasons* of the year. There are festivals in winter, spring, summer, and fall.

Italians eat special foods at these times of year because many vegetables and fruits grow during only one season.

Tomatoes grow only in summer. Festivals that happen in June, July, and August feature meals with tomatoes. There are so many tomatoes that no one can eat them all! At the end of summer, people use their extra tomatoes to make tomato sauce. They put the sauce into glass jars and save it

Two Italian women make their own tomato sauce.

in their *pantry*. That way, they can eat tomatoes all year long.

Many festivals and celebrations in Italy are religious. They are *Catholic* (KATH-lick) holidays. The Roman Catholic Church is very important in

St. Peter's Cathedral is the Catholic church in Vatican City.

Italy. The head of the Church is called the Pope. He lives in a special place in Italy called Vatican (VAH-tih-kun) City. It is located in the capital city of Rome.

There are many *saints* in the Catholic religion. Saints are people who were very good during their lives. Some saints died a long time ago but are still remembered for their goodness. People ask the saints to watch out for them and to help them.

Each saint is famous for a special thing. Saint Francis of Assisi is the saint of animals. Every year on Saint Francis's Day, people bring their dogs, cats, birds, and other animals to church.

Italians celebrate the birthdays of saints. They make special foods on these days. You will be reading about one saint, Saint Joseph, who is famous for helping the poor. Try some of the recipes prepared on his day.

Italians have the secret to a good life. To make people happy, you have to make their stomachs happy. See if you can make your stomach happy!

Saint Joseph's Day

Many cities and regions in Italy have a *patron saint* (PAY-trun saynt). This saint watches over the city. People pray to the patron saint when they wish for things to happen. A boy might pray for his mother to get well when she is sick.

People on the island of Sicily celebrate many saints. One saint that all of Sicily celebrates is Saint Joseph. He was the husband of Mary, the mother of Jesus. He lived two thousand years ago. Italians believe that Saint Joseph protects their homes and families.

Saint Joseph is the saint of the poor. Each year, Saint Joseph's Day is celebrated on March 19th. On this day, poor people are helped, just like Joseph would do if he were alive. This festival takes place at the beginning of spring.

People in Sicily make a Saint Joseph's Day table.

Sicily

Sicily is an island in the middle of the *Mediterranean Sea* (meh-duh-tuh-RAY-nee-un see). Sicily was invaded by armies from different *cultures* (KULL-churz). People wanted this beautiful island because many fruits and vegetables grow easily there. Also, it is close to the continents of Africa and Europe. The people who live on Sicily are called Sicilians (suh-SILL-yunz). They are very proud of their island. They are Italian but like to call themselves Sicilian instead. Many people who live on Sicily speak both Italian and a language called Sicilian. Sicilians still make foods that came from the cultures who invaded the island many years ago.

People prayed to Saint Joseph when the volcano Mount Etna erupted in 1981. An artist made this statue of him after their city was saved.

This long table is covered with all kinds of food. Saint Joseph's Day tables are found in people's houses and also in the center of towns and cities. Some Italians who have moved to the United States or other countries make Saint Joseph's Day tables too.

Italians also create bread altars. A bread altar is a raised platform where gifts are left for the saints. Sicilians build the altars out of wood and metal. All week long, people bake loaves of bread in all kinds of shapes. This bread is not for eating. It is only for decoration.

Some bread is made to look like Saint Joseph. Other bread is woven to look like a basket. Some breads are made into the shape of a boat or a fish. Also on the altar are candles and pictures of Joseph.

Many bean dishes are served on Saint Joseph's Day because they grow during spring. There are many types of beans, like *fava beans* and *chickpeas*.

On the morning of Saint Joseph's Day, people

walk from house to house. They taste food from all the Saint Joseph's Day tables. In the afternoon, the *priest* comes from the local church to give a *blessing* for the tables.

There is so much food on the Saint Joseph's Day tables so that all the poor people can eat from it. When everyone sits down at the table, people yell out, "Long live Saint Joseph!" At the end of the meal, everyone takes home a loaf of bread from the bread altar. The loaf stays in the house for a year. It is supposed to bring good luck.

Chickpeas

Chickpeas are a kind of round bean. They are also called garbanzo (gar-BON-zo) beans. Their name in Latin means "small ram" because they look like a ram's head. Chickpeas are eaten all over Italy. They are *harvested* in spring and eaten fresh. Italians pick chickpeas and leave them out to dry. These dried beans can be stored and eaten all year long. They last more than a year in the pantry. To eat dried chickpeas, cover the beans with water in a bowl overnight.

Fried Cream Puffs

2 teaspoons of lemon zest

3 eggs

2 tablespoons of sugar

1 pound of ricotta cheese

1 cup of flour

4 teaspoons of baking powder

salt

2 cups of vegetable oil

1/4 cup of powdered sugar

- Scrub the outside of a lemon. Lightly rub the skin on a grater to make the lemon zest.

- Crack the eggs into a bowl. Beat them lightly with a fork.

- Add the sugar, ricotta cheese, flour, baking powder, lemon zest, and some salt. Mix together well.

- Cover and refrigerate for 1 hour.

- Pour about 3 inches of oil into a large saucepan over medium-high heat. Wait about 7 minutes. Drop 3 or 4 spoonfuls of batter into the oil.

- Turn them over so both sides turn golden brown.

- Remove the fried puffs with a slotted spoon or a pair of tongs. Place them on a paper towel to drain.

- Cut into a puff. The oil was not hot enough if the center is still wet. Let it get hotter before dropping in more batter.

- Repeat with the rest of the batter.

- Sprinkle with powdered sugar. Makes about 32 puffs.

Rice and Lentils

1 cup of instant white rice

1 stalk of celery

1 carrot

1 onion

2 cups of lentils

salt

1/4 cup of olive oil

pepper

1 bunch of Italian parsley

◆ Cook the rice according to the package directions. Set it aside.

◆ Chop the celery, carrot, and onion into small pieces.

◆ Put the lentils, celery, onion, carrot, and some salt into a large saucepan. Fill the pan with 1 inch of water. Bring to a *boil*.

- Cover the pan. Turn the heat to low. Cook for 35 minutes.

- Stir in the rice and olive oil. Sprinkle pepper on top.

- Chop the parsley. Add it on top. Serves 6.

Romaine Salad with Fennel

1 head of romaine lettuce

1/2 head of fennel

1/2 onion

1/4 cup of olive oil

1 lemon

salt and pepper

- Pull the leaves off the head of romaine. Stack them and cut into strips.

- Cut the stalks off the fennel. Cut the bulb into thin slices.

- Cut the onion into small pieces.

- Combine the lettuce, fennel, and onion in a bowl. Add the olive oil.

- Cut the lemon in half. Stick a fork into the middle. Twist it around over the bowl to squeeze the juice out.

- Sprinkle on some salt and pepper.

- Mix with two forks. Serves 4.

Romaine Salad with Fennel

Christmas

Christmas is the holiday for remembering the birth of *Jesus Christ.* Catholics and other Christians believe that Jesus died for people's sins and came back to life. He brought messages of love and kindness to the world. His birthday is celebrated on December 25th. Christmas is not just one day in Italy. It lasts a whole month. Italians have the biggest feast on Christmas Eve, the night before Christmas.

Italians *fast* on the day before Christmas. Fasting

This nativity scene is set up in a public square in Rome.

means not eating some kinds of foods. Sometimes a person who is fasting does not eat anything at all. On Christmas Eve, Italians have a large feast to break the fast. This is where the term "breakfast" comes from. The morning meal breaks the fast that you had overnight.

The feast on Christmas Eve is called the Feast of Seven Fishes. This tradition began in the 7th century, over 1,400 years ago. Seven fish dishes are served.

Fish was prepared because meat was expensive.

Pope John Paul II leads the Midnight Mass on Christmas in St. Peter's Cathedral.

Also, the fish is a symbol for Christianity in the Bible. The *Bible* is the holy book for Christians. Catholics also eat fish during their fast because they are not allowed to eat meat.

There are many reasons for the number 7 in the Feast of Seven Fishes. One is that there are seven days of the week. Another is that there are seven hills around Rome.

Every dish is served one at a time. The dinner can take a long time! After dinner, people go to church for *Midnight Mass*. This Catholic service starts at midnight on Christmas Eve.

Nativity (nuh-TIH-vuh-tee) scenes are set up all over Italy. A nativity scene shows the birth of Jesus. It has statues of Jesus as a baby and of Mary and Joseph. Statues of animals, shepherds, and kings called the Three Wise Men are also set up. Some scenes are life-sized. Others have tiny figures, like dolls.

In some regions of Italy, gifts are given on Christmas Day. But many children get presents

The Christmas Season

In Italy, the Christmas season starts on December 5th. This day is the Feast of Saint Nicholas. Children leave their shoes near their beds. If they have been good, Saint Nicholas leaves a little box of candy in their shoes. December 13th is Saint Lucy's Day. She is the saint of lights. People light torches and fires and hang lights to honor her. The season ends on January 6th when La Befana flies on her broomstick to every child's house to deliver presents.

on January 6th. An old lady named *La Befana* (bay-FAH-nah) comes. She rides around on a broomstick and hands out gifts. La Befana leaves toys and gifts for good children. Bad children get lumps of garlic mixed with licorice that look like coal.

There are many different kinds of fishes in Italy. The main fish that is served during Christmas Eve dinner is *eel*. Eels look like long, black snakes. They live in the ocean. Not everyone eats eels. You can still taste Christmas in Italy, even without the eel.

Spaghetti with Clams

salt

16 ounces of spaghetti

1/4 cup of olive oil

3 cloves of garlic

1 pound of canned minced clams
   (two small cans)

1/4 cup of bread crumbs

1 bunch of Italian parsley

pepper

- Fill a large saucepan 3/4 full with water. Add a *pinch* of salt.

- Add the spaghetti when the water comes to a boil. Cook for 12 minutes. Drain. Save about 1/4 cup of the spaghetti water in another bowl.

- Chop the cloves of garlic into small pieces. Put the olive oil and garlic into a large skillet over medium-high heat.

- Add the canned clams when the garlic turns golden brown. Stir for 3 minutes. Add the spaghetti water.

- Turn the heat down to medium-low. Cover and cook for 10 minutes, until half of the water is gone.

- Add the bread crumbs and the pasta. Stir.
- Chop the parsley into small pieces. Sprinkle it on top.

- Sprinkle salt and pepper on top. Serves 4.

Spaghetti with Clams and Sautéed Shrimp

Sautéed Shrimp

2 pounds of shelled, frozen jumbo shrimp
3 cloves of garlic
1/4 cup of olive oil
1 lemon
pepper
1 bunch of Italian parsley

- Thaw the shrimp overnight in the refrigerator or in a bowl of cold running water.

- Chop the garlic into small pieces. Put the garlic and olive oil in a large skillet over medium-high heat.

- Add the shrimp when the garlic turns golden.

- Stir. The shrimp are done when they turn solid white. Be careful not to overcook them. Put the shrimp into a bowl.

◆ Cut the lemon in half. Squeeze both halves over the shrimp.

◆ Sprinkle some pepper on top.

◆ Chop the parsley into small pieces. Sprinkle it on top. Serves 6.

Eggplant and Tuna Salad

1 large eggplant
salt
1 small onion
1 large can or 2 small cans of tuna
1/4 cup of olive oil
4 tablespoons of red wine vinegar
pepper

4 large slices of bread, sourdough or wheat

◆ Preheat the oven to 400 degrees.

◆ Cut the eggplant in half. Sprinkle a
  pinch of salt on both halves. Place the
  eggplant into a glass baking dish or onto
  a cookie sheet. Bake for 20 minutes,
  until a fork slides through the eggplant
  easily.

◆ Scoop out the insides of the eggplant
  into a bowl. Throw out the skin.

◆ Chop the onion into small pieces. Add it
  to the bowl.

◆ Stir in the canned tuna, olive oil, and
  vinegar. Sprinkle some pepper on top.
  Stir.

◆ Toast the bread slices. Spoon some of
  the eggplant-tuna mixture on top of
  each piece of toast. Serves 4.

The Festival of Santa Rosalia

Palermo (puh-LAIR-mo) is the largest city on the island of Sicily. In July, the whole city comes alive for the Festival of Santa Rosalia. This festival is in the middle of summer. It lasts for six days.

Summer foods like tomatoes, watermelon, and ice cream are eaten during the feasts. People also eat a mixture of toasted nuts, sunflower seeds, and squash seeds. Small snails are cooked with garlic and sold on the street. People suck the snails out of their shells as they walk through town.

Saint Rosalia is the patron saint of Palermo. Sicilians believe that she saved the city from a *plague* (PLAYG). Rosalia died in 1159. She lived in a large cave outside the city of Palermo away from all people.

In 1624, almost 500 years later, the people of Palermo were dying from the plague. The disease spread quickly from family to family. Many people died. One night, a man had a dream in which Saint

Italians in Palermo leave flowers, candles, and other offerings at a shrine for Saint Rosalia.

Rosalia spoke to him. She told him to get her bones from the cave where she died. She told the man to carry them through the city. After he did this, people stopped dying from the plague.

Since then, Saint Rosalia has been honored for saving Palermo. Each year on July 15th, Sicilians have a week of parades. They carry Saint Rosalia's bones through the streets. People make ribbons, flags, and banners with her picture on it.

On the sixth night, fireworks are set off. The sky and the whole sea are lit up with the fireworks. The town comes out to watch.

The summer in Sicily is very hot. Sicilians do not wake up until the late morning. They take a nap for three hours in the middle of the day. All the shops close. Then the people stay up late to enjoy the cooler nights. On festival days, people eat and drink late into the night. On Saint Rosalia's Day, people celebrate by making ice desserts with fruits that are in season.

Every day in Italy, and on Saint Rosalia's Day,

Olives

Olives are fruit that come from trees. Some olive trees in Italy may be over 1,000 years old! Olives are very popular in Italy. They are picked between September and December. People hit the trees with large sticks so that all the olives fall onto the ground. The olives are pressed by large wheels to make olive oil. Olive oil is used for cooking in Italy. Olives are also left whole and *cured* in salt and water for six weeks or more. Then they are put into jars and stored in the pantry. That way, they can be eaten all year.

people eat *pasta* (PAHS-tah). Pasta is made from flour and eggs. It is cut into hundreds of different shapes, as many as you can dream up. Spaghetti (spuh-GEH-tee) is a kind of pasta. Pasta is often eaten with tomato sauce. It is also eaten with all kinds of fresh vegetables. Sometimes it is eaten with a little oil. It is easy to make your own pasta. Just follow the recipe in this book.

Milk and Nut Pudding

4 cups of whole milk

1/2 cup and 2 tablespoons of cornstarch

1/2 cup of sugar

1/4 cup of chocolate chips

1/4 cup of slivered or chopped almonds

- Put the milk and cornstarch into a saucepan. Turn the heat to low. Stir with a wire whisk until all the lumps are out.

- Add the sugar.

- Keep stirring until the mixture comes to a boil. Let it boil for 1 minute, then turn off the heat.

- Pour the mixture into 4 small mugs or glasses. Refrigerate for 1 hour.

- Sprinkle the chocolate chips and almonds onto the pudding. Serves 4.

Mazzarino Salad

1/2 small cabbage

3 carrots

1 green or red apple

1 orange or 2 tangerines

1 lemon

1/2 cup of olive oil

salt and pepper

◆ Remove the hard core from the center of the cabbage. Chop the cabbage into thin strips.

◆ Chop the carrots into small pieces.

◆ Cut the apple in half. Remove the core, stem, and seeds. Chop the apple into small pieces.

◆ Peel the orange or tangerines. Slice into small pieces.

- Put the cabbage, carrots, apple, and orange into a mixing bowl.

- Cut the lemon in half. Squeeze the juice of both halves over the salad.

- Add the olive oil. Stir.

- Sprinkle on some salt and pepper. Refrigerate for at least 1/2 hour. Serves 4.

Lemon Granita
(lemon ice dessert)

4 cups of water
1 1/2 cup of sugar
1 teaspoon of lemon zest
1 cup of fresh lemon juice, from about 4 lemons

- Put the water and sugar into a saucepan on medium heat. Stir until the sugar dissolves.

- Boil for 5 minutes to make a syrup. Take the pan off the heat to cool.

- Scrub the outside of one lemon. Lightly rub the skin on a grater to make the lemon zest.

- Cut all the lemons in half. Squeeze them on a juicer. Or stick a fork into a lemon half and twist. Let the juice drip into a bowl.

- Add the lemon juice and zest to the syrup.

- Pour the mixture into a metal cake pan or a wide metal bowl. Put it in the freezer.

- Stir every 30 minutes for at least 2 hours. This will break up the ice crystals.

- The crystals harden to make a slush. Pour into small glasses. Serves 6.

Homemade Spaghetti with Tomato Sauce and Lemon Granita

Homemade Spaghetti with Tomato Sauce

You need a large work space to make pasta. Make sure your entire counter is clean.

Spaghetti

4 cups of unbleached all-purpose flour
5 extra-large eggs

- Pile the flour into a mound on a large cutting board. Make a hole in the middle. Crack the eggs into the hole. Mix them into the flour with your hands.

- Form the dough into a ball. Press it with your fists. Fold the edges into the center. Grab the dough and push it through your fingers. Knead until the dough turns light yellow and becomes smooth.

- Form the dough into a ball. Wrap in plastic and refrigerate for at least 1 hour.

- Unwrap the ball. Cut it into 4 equal pieces. Keep one piece out for rolling. Cover the rest and put them back into the refrigerator.

- Sprinkle flour onto a counter or cutting board. Flatten the dough into a square with your hand.

- Wipe flour onto a rolling pin. Roll the dough out into a very thin sheet. Sprinkle flour on top.

- Cut the dough into very thin strips.

Pick up the strips and shake them. Sprinkle more flour on the strips. Separate them into a loose pile to dry.

- Repeat with the other 3 pieces of dough.

- Bring a large pot of water to a boil. Drop in the spaghetti. Cook for about 4 minutes. Drain.

- Scoop the spaghetti into bowls. Pour sauce on top (see the following recipe). Serves 4.

Tomato Sauce

2 cloves of garlic

3 tablespoons of olive oil

2 14-ounce cans or 1 28-ounce can of chopped, peeled tomatoes

oregano

salt and pepper

4 leaves of fresh basil

- Chop the garlic into small pieces.

- Pour the olive oil into a large skillet over medium-high heat. Add the garlic.

- Add the tomatoes when the garlic turns golden brown.

- Sprinkle in some oregano, salt, and pepper.

- Chop the basil leaves into pieces. Stir them into the sauce.

- Cook for 15 minutes.

- Serve on top of spaghetti.

Glossary

Bible: a holy book that Christians, Jews, and Muslims believe tells the story of God.

blessing: an act by a god or religious leader that makes something holy.

boil: to heat water or another liquid until it starts to bubble.

Catholic: a member of the branch of the Christian religion called the Roman Catholic Church.

chickpeas: small, yellowish beans that are eaten throughout the Mediterranean. They are also called garbanzo beans.

continent: a large body of land separated from other bodies of land by an ocean or sea. There are seven continents in the world.

culture: a set of behaviors—including food, music, and clothing—that is typical of a group of people.

cured: a process of preserving foods for later use.

Olives are cured in salt or chemicals. They will not spoil for many years.

eel: a long fish that lives in the ocean and some lakes. It looks like a snake.

espresso: strong coffee that is usually served in very small cups.

Europe: a continent with such countries as Italy, France, Germany, Hungary, and Switzerland.

fast: the act of not eating anything or not eating certain foods, like meat. Fasting is usually done for religious reasons.

fava beans: large beans that grow in a large, thick pod. They must be shelled two times before you can eat them.

harvest: the time of year when foods are ripe and ready to be picked.

Jesus Christ: the founder of the Western religion called Christianity. He was born near Jerusalem two thousand years ago.

La Befana: a witch who delivers presents to Italian children on January 6th.

Mediterranean Sea: the body of water between Europe and Africa. It reaches from the coast of Spain to the coast of Israel.

Midnight Mass: a Catholic religious service held at midnight the day before Easter and the day before Christmas.

pantry: a part of the kitchen for keeping canned foods and dry foods, like cereal and rice.

pasta: noodles made from flour and eggs that are used in Italian cooking.

patron saint: a saint who is believed to watch over a specific city or area.

pinch: the amount that you can pick up with your first finger and thumb.

plague: a disease that spreads across a large group of people. It often causes death.

priest: a leader in some branches of Christianity, such as the Roman Catholic Church.

saints: special people remembered in the Catholic religion for their goodness.

season: one of the four parts of the year—spring, summer, winter, and fall. Each season has a different kind of weather and different fruits and vegetables that become ripe.

Bibliography

Allen, Derek. *Italy*. Austin, Tex.: Raintree Steck-Vaughn, 1996.

Angell, Carole S. *Celebrations Around the World: A Multicultural Handbook*. Golden, Colo.: Fulcrum Press, 1996.

Bell, Rachael. *A Visit to Italy*. Des Plaines, Ill.: Heinemann Library, 1999.

Blashfield, Jean F. *Italy*. New York: Children's Press, 1999.

Hausam, Josephine Sander. *Italy*. Milwaukee: Gareth Stevens, 1999.

Kindersley, Anabel, and Barnabas Kindersley. *Celebrations: Festivals, Carnivals, and Feast Days from*

Around the World. New York: DK Publishing, 1997.

Martin, Fred. *Italy.* Des Plaines, Ill.: Heinemann Library, 1999.

Ridgwell, Jenny. *A Taste of Italy.* Austin, Tex.: Raintree Steck-Vaughn, 1993.

Vezza, Simone. *Passport on a Plate: A Round-the-World Cookbook for Children.* New York: Simon & Schuster, 1997.

Webb, Lois Sinaiko. *Holidays of the World Cookbook for Students.* Phoenix, Ariz.: Oryx Press, 1995.

websites:

http://www.initaly.com/~initaly/travel/info/events.htm

http://italianculture.miningco.com

Index